FOR LOVE OF THE
Clydesdale Hor

Heidi M Sands

Old Pond
PUBLISHING LTD

First published 2017

Copyright © Heidi M Sands, 2017

ISBN 9781912158126

Old Pond Publishing
5m Enterprises,
8 Smithy Wood Drive,
Sheffield,
S35 1QN, UK

www.oldpond.com

All photographs and text
are by Heidi M Sands

Book design by Liz Whatling
Printed and bound in India

Introduction

The Clydesdale horse has its origins in eighteenth century Lanarkshire, taking its name from the area once known as Clydesdale. Two men, the Sixth Duke of Hamilton and John Paterson of Lochlyloch, are credited with establishing the breed, bringing Flemish stallions into the area in an attempt to improve local native horses by cross-breeding. Success followed and these improved horses formed the backbone of the breed we know today as the Clydesdale.

These horses ultimately spread beyond Lanarkshire to become Scotland's real 'horsepower', being used in both town and countryside situations. At its height it is estimated that the breed numbered in the region of 140,000 pure and cross-bred horses.

The Clydesdale was not only the pride of Scotland, however, he was exported over the border to England and found himself overseas in growing numbers too, in particular in Australia, New Zealand, North and South America and Canada.

By the 1950s, however, the Clydesdale had had his heyday. Increasing use of tractors and the internal combustion engine saw him superseded for farm work and for use in Scotland's urban environment. Some say this revolution was speeded up, particularly in the countryside, by the arrival of grass sickness, a killer disease that still today causes the untimely death of horses in areas where it is prevalent.

By the mid-1970s the Clydesdale's numbers were so low that it was recognised by the Rare Breeds Survival Trust as being 'vulnerable' and categorised as such. Today numbers have stabilised, although the breed is still recognised as being rare.

The Clydesdale horse makes a huge impression on those who appreciate and work with him. His huge size; he stands at around 17hh, makes him unmissible, his striking good looks turn heads wherever he goes and his ability to adapt to his place in the twenty-first century endear him to horse-lovers worldwide.

He is a true gentle giant; gentle enough for the youngest child to be introduced to, yet strong enough to pull a heavily laden dray. He is also adaptable and capable of being ridden in competition or for pleasure. He can on occasion jump, although it may not be very high, and he has also been used for logging duties where mechanical means are not suitable. He is most of all though a lovely horse, and from humble Scottish farm horse the Clydesdale has come far.

Each year at the prestigious Royal Highland Show at Ingliston, Edinburgh, the Clydesdale horse wows audiences with his in-hand performances and driven ability; elsewhere he shines out under saddle. His power is revered, his gentleness renowned and the way in which he turns his hoof to almost any task is a credit to the men and women who have kept this great Scottish icon to the fore.

Nowhere is this more noticeable than in Aberdeenshire at Strathorn Farm Stables, home of George and Ruth Skinner, for it's here that Clydesdales are taught to perform as a drill team to music, the sight of which simply cannot fail to impress. Not only that but Strathorn horses are ridden

Strathorn stables.

side-saddle, pull drays and enter private driving classes, proving if proof were needed that the Clydesdale really can be the perfect all-rounder.

Over the last thirty years I've been lucky enough to observe the Clydesdale horse in action and to get to know him, to photograph him in different situations and to speak to those who know him best, including Wendy Lynn Cristante, owner and proprietor of the former 'Canadian Clyde Ride'. Based in British Columbia, Canada, Wendy began riding her first Clydesdales in the early 2000s as a way of exercising them. Impressed by the ability of this heavy horse under saddle and the way in which he followed commands, Wendy gathered a team of liked-minded women and Clydesdale horses around her, training and teaching the world's first heavy horse musical ride to literally dance to music. Fame followed, culminating in appearances at the world-famous Calgary Stampede.

Not to be outdone, and in the same time frame in the UK, ten Clydesdale horses from the former 'West Highland Heavy Horses' relocated from Scotland's Isle of Skye to Cumbria's Duddon Valley to become 'Cumbrian Heavy Horses'. Nothing strange there you might think, except that these horses didn't travel by horsebox or lorry, they travelled on foot, or should that be hoof, every inch of the 420 miles, being ridden by teams of altering riders on the 'Great Clydesdale Migration'.

Although unable to record either of these graphic Clydesdale moments photographically, my appetite was whetted for what images this magnificent breed could inspire. Thus the idea for *For Love of the Clydesdale Horse* was born, and when Old Pond asked if I had another book in me, it was easy to see the direction that book would take.

For Love of the Clydesdale Horse is not a breed bible, it was never meant to be. It does not contain standards or lists of stallions at stud, what it is is a photographic celebration of the Clydesdale horse in his working clothes, with his show suit on or going about his daily business. The photographs are not staged, they simply happened at that moment in time and I hope they are none the worse for that.

If like me you admire Scotland's only native heavy horse then I hope you will enjoy this book. For me it's been a privilege to observe the Clydesdale in this way, to choose which photographs to include and to pore over them. Many photographs were discarded, sadly not all could be included and due to geographical and time constraints not all events and happenings could be attended or photographed.

In summing up; Scotland is a stunning country, come and see for yourself if you are not lucky enough to live here. In its fields, stables, steadings and show-rings one of its most famous icons, the Clydesdale horse, lives out its life, unaware of just how magnificent he really is. His huge feathered feet, his calm unflappable nature, his inquisitive outlook and his place in history will ensure his longevity for generations to come, and I for one, am delighted at that.

Ploughing matches are one way to teach the next generation of enthusiasts the way to work the Clydesdale horse.

The Heritage of the Working Clydesdale

Scotland owes a debt of gratitude to the Clydesdale; the country's only native heavy horse. He was once the real horsepower, pulling all manner of horse-drawn vehicles and implements in both town and countryside situations. In the early twentieth century all that changed; the internal combustion engine took over and more or less consigned this magnificent working animal to memory. Until, of course, more recent times when enthusiasts of the breed resurrected and re-adopted that working ability. Today this can be seen in a variety of situations, including at shows, ploughing matches and displays in Scotland and elsewhere.

Ploughing matches are held during the winter months. It may be cold, dull and the days are short but fields of stubble, left for the purpose of ploughing, entice ploughmen and their horses to pit their skills against one another to see just who can plough the straightest furrow.

Throughout the better months of the year the Clydesdale is to be found at summer shows pulling drays, farm carts and other vehicles. He is turned out to perfection, as is his vehicle, some of which may have been restored to full working order from barn finds. It's not uncommon for original horse-drawn vehicles to still turn up at farm sales or be found in the backs of barns or buildings, much to the delight of restorers.

Keeping this noble breed working, in whatever way, harks back to the past. It's also a way of ensuring a future and passing on valuable skills of horsemanship that may otherwise be lost.

Horse brasses adorn the collar.

Following a pair through plough is hard work requiring skill.

Extra help and guidance may be needed.

Mixed pairs may be seen. Note one horse down on the plough, the other on the stubble.

Running repairs or alterations may be needed.

In working attire.

It's important to plough a straight furrow and this takes real concentration and control.

The end result.

Blinkers are used on heavy horse bridles to keep the horse's mind on the job in hand, distractions are not needed.

Farm carts come in different shapes and sizes depending on the part of the country they originate from, their exact usage and the craftsman's skill.

The high-peaked collar, a Scottish tradition.

Harness comes in different styles, show harness must be cleaned to perfection and be an exact fit.

The Co-operative single horse turnout.

Manners must be perfect before setting foot in the show-ring and it takes hours of work to get to this standard.

Clydesdales must be able to trot out and cover the ground.

A well-matched pair.

*The Millisle
Clydesdale
turnout.*

Attention to detail includes the paint work on vehicles. Master craftsmen complete this type of work in time-honoured fashion.

At the Royal Highland Show.

A groom is on hand to hold the horse in readiness for the judge to make his appraisal.

Handlers and drivers often adopt a style of dress to complement the type of vehicle that they drive.

Leading a class around the ring.

There is no finer sight in the evening sunshine.

Even the horse's comforts have been thought of. Buckets and nosebags hang from the vehicle.

Focused on his job.

Piles of old working harness still turn up at farm sales or roups. Such items are eagerly sought after.

Detailing is dependent on the saddler who painstakingly created the harness.

Harness resting on a stack stand. These stands were used to keep vermin from accessing the stacked crop.

Demonstration days present an opportunity to see Clydesdales at work.

A pensive moment at the Royal Northern Spring Show, Aberdeenshire.

In the Public Eye

The Clydesdale horse turns heads wherever he goes and nowhere is that more true than in the show-ring. Turned out to perfection, preened, cosseted and bedecked with harness or decoration, he is a magnificent horse. But this magnificence takes time, effort and patience to produce.

Hours of preparation go into making a Clydesdale horse look his best and ready to take his place in the public eye. Grooming, washing, bandaging and a proliferation of talcum powder ensure that his whites are white and that his coat shines with health. That's not all it takes to get this gentle giant into show-ring condition, though.

From an early age the Clydesdale horse needs to be taught manners; first from his mother and other herd members and then from his human handlers. He needs to learn to stand when required, to walk correctly, to turn when asked and to reverse or back up. If he's to be used in harness then his education will start by learning to long-rein, an art in itself, and above all he must be at ease around others, both human and equine.

Onlookers deserve to see only the best that the breed can offer and the best of the best can be seen in June each year at the prestigious Royal Highland Show at Ingliston, Edinburgh. Here Clydesdale horses take centre stage and can be seen both in-hand and under harness.

Elsewhere in more local show-rings and displays this noble horse acquits itself to the highest standard. Take time to stand and watch awhile, the breed is worth the wait.

The Royal Highland Show attracts only the best and here a foal learns from its mother just what is expected.

It can take years of practice to perfect the art of Clydesdale showing.

All lined up for stock judging in Aberdeenshire; see the different tail lengths denoting the age or use of the horse.

Preparations for showing are all important, as here at the Northumberland County Show.

Horsepower turned out to perfection.

The Champion at Northumberland County Show about to take his place in the Grand Parade.

At the Royal Highland Show a youngster has the final check over.

It's important to ensure that all is in place before entering the ring.

An absolutely resplendent turnout, a reflection of the Canadian origins of the vehicle. Note the wide-brimmed Stetsons in keeping with the turnout.

Talcum powder is used in profusion to ensure whiteness of legs and feather.

Many Clydesdales have their tails traditionally decorated for the show-ring.

Putting the flights in by hand to decorate the horse's mane takes time and practice.

The finished mane.

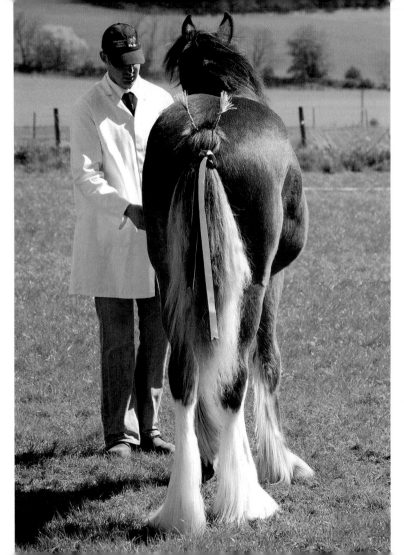

A youngster learns to stand quietly to be shown and evaluated.

Learning how to walk out and behave at home is all-important. It stands young horses in good stead for the future.

The sign says it all: 'The Heavy Horse Wash Area' of the Royal Highland Show, where water is king and stepladders may be needed to get to those hard-to-reach areas.

A thorough clean is necessary to look your best but the soap can get everywhere.

Once soaped everything must be washed off and using a hosepipe is one of the best ways to get the job done.

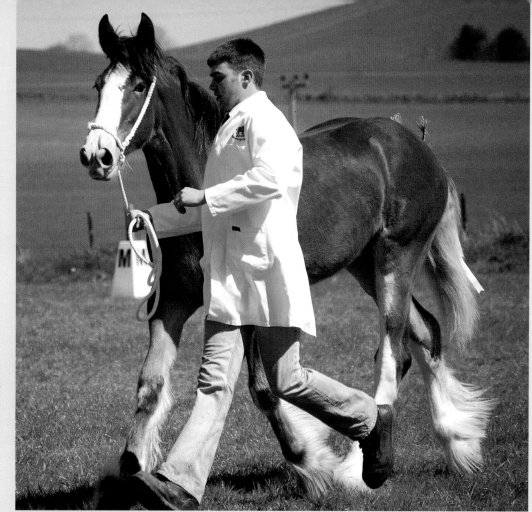

Youngsters need to be taught how to be trotted up for the judge.

Even foals need to be cleaned up in readiness for the show-ring but Mum's close by to offer a reassuring presence.

Every inch needs a good washing and to keep themselves dry handlers may choose to wear wet weather gear.

Power washers come in handy for washing dirt out of heavy-feathered legs.

This mare has her foal at foot and while he may not know it he is already learning from her example.

White legs and markings are common and desirable within the breed.

Preparation before entering the show-ring; note the tail bandage and leg bandages, which will all be removed.

Six beautiful single horse turnouts in the evening sun at the Royal Highland Show.

A typically Scottish tail decoration complete with tartan ribbon.

Prize winners parade together at Thainstone near Inverurie in north-east Scotland.

George and Ruth Skinner's unicorn turnout. The unicorn is one of the most difficult formations to drive as the lead horse is out on his own.

The Ridden Clydesdale

The ridden Clydesdale is a relatively new phenomenon – thirty years ago virtually no one would have considered the Clydesdale as a riding horse. He's come a long way.

Today the Clydesdale is ridden in several different styles and disciplines, from general riding horse to side-saddle. The Strathorn Clydesdales of George and Ruth Skinner in Aberdeenshire even have their own drill team, whose attire and displays evolve to reflect modern culture, including the Olympic Games in Rio in 2016.

It pays to remember that this is a breed that has traditionally been used as a draught horse. Pulling has been his forte and the only time he may have been ridden in days of old might have been by a tired horse-boy on the way back from the field after a day's ploughing.

Today all that has changed, in fact it's true to say that the ridden Clydesdale has given the breed another string to its bow with many shows now putting on classes specifically to cater for this growing trend.

He may be a huge horse, but he's also a gentle giant and this is reflected in his general demeanour and willingness to accept and accommodate a rider on his back. Well-ridden and trained the Clydesdale is a delight to see.

In response to this desire to saddle up and ride the Clydesdale, tack and saddlery have become available for these huge horses. Not only that, if you've a mind you can take the opportunity to try riding a Clydesdale for yourself at several UK riding establishments.

Waiting to go into the ridden class at Keith Show in Banffshire.

*Stylish at
the trot.*

A good walk is essential in the show-ring.

Canter is not a usual pace for this draught horse breed, so it takes practice to perfect.

Strathorn Clydesdale drill team celebrate H.M. The Queen's reign.

Majestic in more ways than one.

Taking part in the grand parade at Grantown Show in the north-east of Scotland.

Murphy ready to give of his best.

Clydesdale horses need schooling the same as any horse in order to be at their best.

Tacking up before riding.

In-hand work can be an important part of preparation for riding.

Celebrating Rio 2016 with the Strathorn Clydesdales.

The drill team walks out in style, a wonderful sight.

More shows than ever before are putting on classes for ridden Clydesdales, a reflection of just how many are being ridden.

Happy smiles on the lap of honour.

In the show-ring at Keith Show.

Strathorn's display team on home ground and ready to entertain the crowd.

It takes a lot of work and dedication to turn out a team like this.

Strathorn's riders in harmony with each other.

Let's go – taking it up a notch.

Getting up some speed yet maintaining control.

Each horse and rider must train to work as a unit within the team.

A beautiful sight, the Clydesdale really can canter.

An unusual sight – a Clydesdale ridden side-saddle.

Elegance personified – another Strathorn pairing from Aberdeenshire.

Riding side-saddle was once the only option for lady riders. No one could then have envisaged riding such huge horses in this way.

From work horse to ladies mount. This shows the true versatility of the breed.

Absolute perfection such as this can only be achieved when horse and rider are working in harmony.

The Rio team leave the ring to a well-earned round of applause.

Private driving with Ruth Skinner and Wallack at the Turriff Show in north-east Scotland in 2016.

These magnificent horses rest between show classes.

Off Duty

In times gone by most Clydesdale horses would have worked much harder than they do today and a day off, or being 'off duty', would have been rare. That's not to say that these heavy work horses wouldn't have been rested; they would, but full days, or even weeks off work would have been virtually unheard of.

Today being off duty can mean all kinds of things for a Clydesdale horse, from generally relaxing to being out at grass. At grass, or liberty, most horses will be able to graze, feel free to wander about and perhaps take a look over the hedge or mix with their field companions. For some this kind of liberty is open-ended and may mean weeks of freedom. For others turnout is given for part of the day, when not working or stabled. Either way this is a real opportunity to feel the grass under their feet.

Young horses are a delight to watch when off duty. With less cares than older horses they will often interact with their human handlers, especially whilst waiting for Mum to return to them. They may also lie down to rest more readily than older horses and are far more likely to sleep in this way; older horses being more likely to rest whilst standing up.

Between classes at shows Clydesdales may rest a back leg, pull at some hay, wait for their next feed to arrive or simply enjoy the sun on their backs.

These two have just had their 'whites' whitened; note the talcum powder-laden grass.

Andy Simpson from Elgin in Moray with his two youngsters – the bond between man and his horses is obvious.

Behind the scenes at the Royal Highland Show, Edinburgh, a horse is led back to the stabling area.

Waiting for his feed.

Dozing with Mum.

Grazing, the best 'downtime' a horse can get.

Strathorn's Clydesdales in Aberdeenshire on the last run of the day.

*Enjoying
the sun as
they wait.*

In the shade at Turriff Show in north-east Scotland.

Keeping the essential equipment together between classes is important.

Winter shows are sometimes held indoors and cattle pens make ideal temporary stabling.

Young horses may hold on to jackets for security, older ones may simply be checking for treats.

This attractive youngster takes a bite of hay whilst waiting.

Learning from the older generation.

Preparation under way, but at the moment this big lad is off duty.

In the evening sun this marvellous Clydesdale comes to call.

This heavy horse will happily share his grazing with several cattle.

Spats are often used to protect the Clydesdale's feathers between show-ring classes.

Watching everything intently.

Offering reassurance and companionship to a young foal.

Mum's back – time for a drink.

*Unusual colouring
sometimes goes along
with blue eyes, as here.*

Resting at Thainstone Agricultural Centre in winter sunshine.

Away we go.

Tail decorations out – it's time to go home.

Cross-bred Clydesdales can be quite spectacular.

Resting together.

Showing can be tiring.

Taking some of Mum's hay.

Heidi M Sands

For more than three decades Heidi M. Sands has lived and worked in the north-east of Scotland, writing and photographing her way through the stronghold of Scotland's only native heavy horse, the Clydesdale. Currently contributing to UK agricultural and equine publications, Heidi has been privileged to photographically record this gentle giant of the horse world at work, rest and play.

Born and brought up in the north-west of England, Heidi studied art and design, including photography at Lancashire's Blackpool and Fylde College and the former Preston Polytechnic. A lifelong horsewoman and award-winning writer, this will be her third title for Old Pond.

Old Pond
PUBLISHING

Founded in 1998 and now owned by 5m Publishing, Old Pond specialises in books and DVDs for the land-based industries from farm machinery and animal breeds to earthmoving, trucking and forestry.

www.oldpond.com

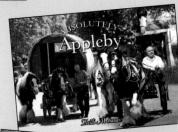

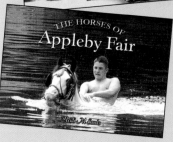